This delightful book is the latest in the series of Ladybird books that have been specially planned to help grown-ups with the world about them.

As in the other books in this series, the large, clear script, the careful choice of words, the frequent repetition and the thoughtful matching of text with pictures all enable grown-ups to think they have taught themselves to cope. The subject of the book will greatly appeal to grown-ups.

Series 999

THE LADYBIRD
BOOKS FOR GROWN-UPS SERIES

THE
HIPSTER

by

J. A. HAZELEY, N.S.F.W. and J. P. MORRIS, O.M.G.

(Authors of 'There Has been a Magnificent Mistake')

Publishers: Ladybird Books Ltd, Loughborough
Printed in England. If wet, Italy.

This is a hipster.

He is childless, unaccountably wealthy, and always well turned out.

He likes art, porridge, scarves, and anything reclaimed from French factories, like this dog rack.

Jinja has opened a pop-up trifle bistro in an old Spitfire.

Every Friday, he DJs in a club where all the furniture has been burned deliberately.

His favourite band today is robofolk duo My Dead Esterházy.

Hipsters like to collect old things that are unfashionable, because that makes them fashionable.

Vintage washing-up bowls are highly prized, because they look neither retro nor valuable, and are therefore both.

Caff Eh? in Brighton is a popular spot for hipsters.

The owner guarantees that his customers will never have heard of anything on the menu – things like dotka, commoner's milk, blacknock and carnip tartonne, keyhole coffee and these freshly oven-balched beetcorn labneys.

Petr runs a micro-still from the basement of a condemned electricity sub-station.

Here he makes craft gin, infused with sausage and toothpaste.

Petr is available as an app.

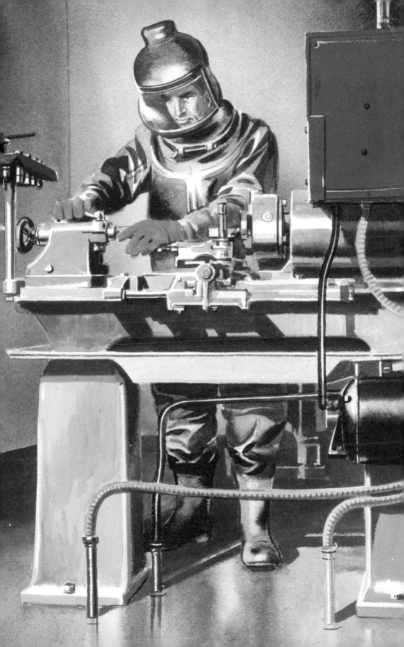

Hipsters like art.

This sculpture, called 'All the Dances I have ever Danced and in the Order I Danced Them', sold for over £11,000,000 at a bespoke car-boot art fair.

It is made of sock.

Niven is a non-linear campaign provocateur for a brandwidth trendship engagement agency.

Like most hipsters, he has no office, and carries his modified electric typewriter from coffee shop to coffee shop, on his motorised unicycle.

He dresses like this all the time.

Hipsters think plates are very old fashioned. They prefer to eat from planks, tiles and first-generation iPads.

This tofu self-identifying cross-species is being served on a spring-loaded folder that contains the script of a short film about a skateboarding shoelace designer.

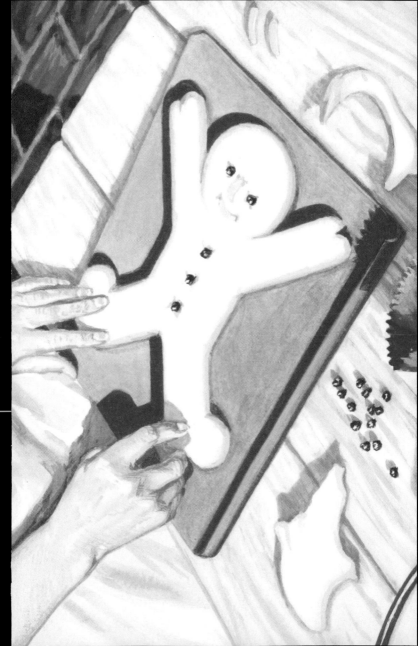

Coffee is the hipster's favourite drink.

These dry espressos are made with baby scallions and chia roots and cost over £8 per cup.

They contain no water.

This is a poster for an event combining scratch cinema and a live performance by The East London Clapping Orchestra.

If you look carefully at it, you can see none of the details.

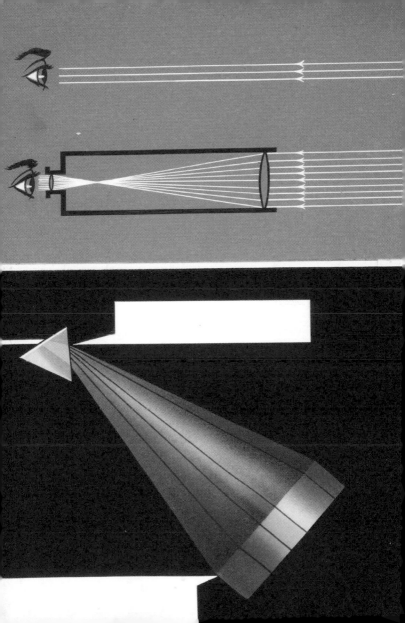

At hipster cocktail kitchen aitcH2ooEau, all the drinks are made with nothing but water.

Here, two mixographers are preparing a Coldplay's Next Album, a cocktail made with fourteen different sorts of water.

The most highly prized water is Japanese fen tears.

Phoo is an action poet. She narrowcasts what she calls "political demo-biography" using vintage technology.

To make it more difficult to find and enjoy her work, she records each performance on to pre-used Betamax cassettes and leaves them in charity shops labelled with the names of unpopular ITV sitcoms on the spine in Dymo Tape.

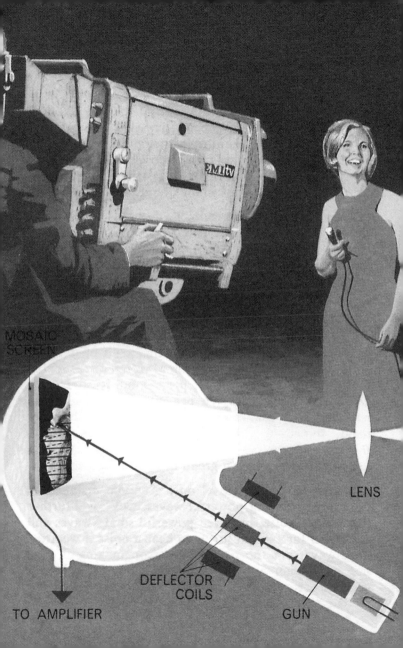

MOSAIC
SCREEN

TO AMPLIFIER

DEFLECTOR
COILS

GUN

LENS

Hipsters like to find places that have not yet been spoiled by mainstream culture – like the sea.

This upcycled boring tower is now the third hippest community in Europe. It has its own calendar, two years ahead of ours.

Tiswas has bought the insides of a lighthouse off eBay. He is installing it in his second-hand shoetique, which he hopes will make an important point.

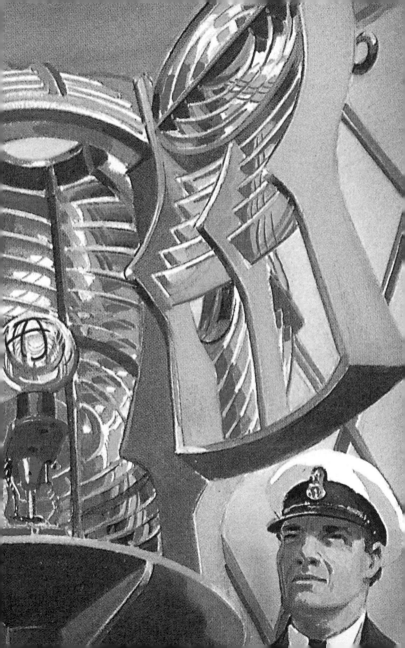

Hipsters like to go clubbing.

At this club, no one dances, but everyone has a shower. There are six different flavours of shower, including bouillon, verbena tea and miso soup.

The floor is coated with smoked glass, so everyone can admire their underneaths.

Jedd's job is to be written about in magazines.

Here he is making a vintage chocolate car, so he can be photographed making a vintage chocolate car.

He will eventually put it up for sale on a website whose address will not work.

Hipsters are always on the look-out for new beards.

These hipsters have travelled to the Arctic Circle to photograph Norwegian fishermen's beards.

One of them is weeing his tag into the snow.

Neena likes to wear hats made of forklift tyres and coloured balls.

This one was designed especially for her by her friend Grayson Perry, who lives in the boat above hers.

What hipsters like best about their favourite music is that nobody really likes it.

This band is currently called Donkiet Cong. They improvise ironictronica based on 1990s weather forecasts, using school instruments and hindsight.

If anyone applauds, they split up and reform in the venue next door with a new name.

Since opening two years ago, Sew:Ho has become an essential stop on the drop-in sewing scene.

Each machine is fitted with a USB port so the ladies can bring their own downloaded thread.

Hipsters like to keep fit. Among their preferred exercise routines are yogaquatics, jitterbugging, and going upside down.

These two men go upside down in special pyjamas you can only buy from a company in Mexico.

At this macromanufactory, Ned the Third and his friends make soup cannons. Hipsters like to cook using cannons, because it takes so very, very long.

This is also why they slow-toast their bread with hairdryers.

Ned the Third has eleven phones.

Hipsters like body art.

Zorro has found this picture he drew as a child. He is going to have it tattooed on to his dog.

It is important to the hipster that things look like other things.

Half of these things are hats. The others are small-batch artisan savoury pastries.

Can you tell which is which?

The authors would like to thank the illustrators whose work they have so mercilessly ribbed, and whose glorious craftsmanship was the set-dressing of their childhoods. The inspiration they sparked has never faded.

MICHAEL JOSEPH

UK | USA | Canada | Ireland | Australia
India | New Zealand | South Africa

Michael Joseph is part of the Penguin Random House group of companies whose addresses can be found at global.penguinrandomhouse.com
First published 2015

007

Printed in Italy by L.E.G.O. S.p.A

A CIP catalogue record for this book is available from the British Library

ISBN: 978–0–718–18359–2

www.greenpenguin.co.uk

MIX
Paper from
responsible sources
FSC® C018179

Penguin Random House is committed to a sustainable future for our business, our readers and our planet. This book is made from Forest Stewardship Council® certified paper.